Wire Wrapping For Total Beginners

Ahmadn F. Hossain

Introduction

Wire wrapping is a fascinating craft that allows you to create beautiful jewelry and accessories using wires and various techniques. To get started, you'll need a set of essential wire wrapping tools, which we'll introduce you to briefly.

One of the primary tools you'll use in wire wrapping is a set of pliers/cutters specifically designed for jewelry making. These tools help you manipulate and cut the wire with precision, ensuring your creations come out just as you envision.

As you delve into wire wrapping, you'll learn various techniques. The simple loop is a foundational skill that allows you to create loops with your wire, perfect for connecting elements in your jewelry designs.

Moving on, you'll explore more advanced techniques like wire-wrapped links, which enable you to connect components in a chain-like fashion, adding intricacy to your designs. The wire-wrapped triangle bail is another technique that's essential for creating pendants and other jewelry pieces.

If you want to incorporate beads into your wire-wrapped designs, you'll learn how to wire wrap around a bead and create a wire-wrapped bead cap. These skills open up a world of possibilities for your jewelry creations.

Briolettes are teardrop-shaped gemstone beads that can add elegance to your designs. You'll discover how to wire wrap a briolette to create stunning pendants and earrings.

For those looking to tackle more advanced projects, the wire herringbone technique offers a unique and intricate pattern for your jewelry. Additionally, you can learn how to craft a flower-style wire-wrapped ring, adding a touch of nature-inspired beauty to your jewelry collection.

Lastly, we'll guide you through the process of wire wrapping a cabochon pendant, allowing you to showcase beautiful gemstones in your designs.

With the knowledge and skills you gain from this wire wrapping guide, you'll be well-equipped to embark on your creative journey in jewelry making. Whether you're a beginner or looking to expand your repertoire, wire wrapping offers endless opportunities for artistic expression.

Contents

Wire packaging is a popular jewelry-making technique that offers varieties of beautiful jewelry designs, without the need for many tools.

These techniques can incorporate anything from gemstone beads, gemstone cabochons to charms, and just pure wirework.

HISTORY

No one knows when or where the ancient art of wire wrapping originated. Egyptian and Phoenician artists are known to have practiced art for more than 5,000 years. It is the only known metal jewel that is created completely without welding or casting. The wire used can be of many different alloys, such as copper, brass, silver, or gold.

The surviving records indicate that jewelry from the 17th and earlier century was made with braids, twists, and knots as part of its design motifs, similar to what you find today.

Certainly jewelry of any kind was rare at that time, but what was available was generally in silver. It was used mainly by traders or someone with some social and monetary position. Many people were farmers and traders, so their jewelry needed to be very wearable and resistant.

Although this art has been lost for a time in history, it reappeared during the Victorian Era, where its popularity surpassed traditional cast jewelry. Over the past 30 years, wire jewelry has continued to increase in popularity due to the uniqueness, flexibility, and the "creative ability" of its artisans.

Using wire is a fun and creative way to make jewelry, and once you've mastered the technique, there's no stopping it! But first, you need to know what tools you need to start with and what each tool is used for.

From wire winding beads, creating jewelry to forming various shapes with wire - you'll find everything you need as you go on with this book.

The beauty of the wire wrapping is that you don't need a lot of tools, so it's an inexpensive way to get into jewelry making before moving on to other techniques, like laying stones.

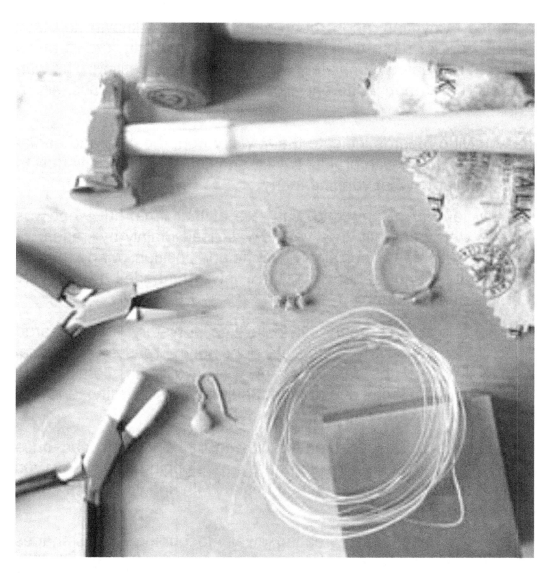

When you start making your jewelry, you will need some basic tools for wrapping jewelry, especially if that particular technique is something you want to get into. Although the beginning stage is very low in terms of what tools you need, there are two ways: you need a few things to proceed.

The good thing is that you don't need much. Of course, as you progress with your jewelry making skills, you will accumulate tons and tons of tools, as I have done over the years as well. You want to learn more techniques, be more creative, learn different ways to wind the yarn, and you will have a few more things. Or maybe one or another company has just launched another set of round-nose pliers that will help you make this basic cycle much easier and rounder.

I have been making jewelry for 13 years and, although I started using beads with beads, I soon learned to wrap wire and never looked back. At the moment, I am learning to start metalworking, but wire wrapping is something that I will always incorporate into most of the jewelry I am making.

A Quick Look At The Basic Wire Wrapping Tools.

I have a lot of wire wrapping tools for making jewelry, so when it came to getting them out of the basics, I went through a difficult time - I use just about everything I have and consider them indispensable.

However, I went back to the time when I started making jewelry and remembered what I needed without the wire wrapping just not working. And this is the list that I created.

Further down, you will find additional tools needed along the way, after discovering that this is the type of jewelry you want to make as a hobby or perhaps as a business at some point.

Meanwhile, here is a quick summary of what you need to know as I go into many details in discussing the various tools in section.

- The first thing you need is wire. Wireless, there's nothing to wrap. When you're starting, copper wire is the best to use, and I'll explain in more detail why. Later, you can also use sterling silver wire when you are ready to start selling your work.
- Pliers. You can never have enough pliers to wrap. However, to begin with, you will need at least a few round nose pliers and chain pliers.
- Cutters. You need to cut the level wire, and a knife or scissors is not what you want here.
- Hammers and mallets. At least a rawhide hammer to strengthen the base frame wire.
- A ruler so you can accurately measure the wire you need to cut for your piece.
- A Sharpie pen or something else to mark the wire for cutting or bending.
- A ring mandrel, if you want to make rings - it is indispensable.
- A bracelet mandrel for making bracelets, preferably oval, but the round will also work.
- Files or files to smooth the sharp edges of the cut wire.

WIRE SELECTION

You cannot begin your adventure in wire rapping without the need for the wire! At first, it can be confusing to know which metal to choose and the correct size. I always recommend practicing with silver or copper-plated wire, as this is economical, so you can switch to silver or gold and, although it is more expensive, it is easier to work with.

You will often see wire measurements in mm or gauge and be able to purchase 10 different sizes in round wires, starting with 0.2 mm (gauge 32) up to 4 mm (gauge 6).

CHOOSE THE RIGHT SIZE WIRE FOR YOUR WIRE WRAPPING PROJECTS

- Wires with 0.2 mm, 0.3 mm, and 0.5 mm are perfect for winding precious stone beads with small to medium holes.
- The 0.6 mm, 0.8 mm, 1 mm wire is great for making your discoveries and forming large shapes.
- The 1.5 mm to 2 mm wire can be used to create rings, bracelets, bracelets, cuffs, and also create frames and structures.
- The 3 mm to 4 mm wire is thick and can be used for bracelets and cuffs, great for robust projects, but it will be more difficult to work with.

WIRE WRAPPING PLIERS/CUTTERS FOR JEWELLERY

- Round Nose Pliers

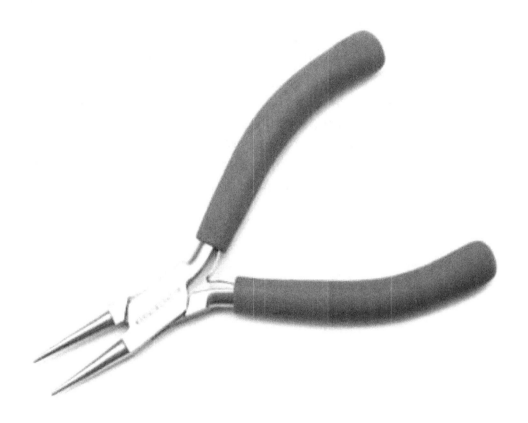

These round nose jewelry pliers are ideal for most jewelry needs and are essential for all types of jewelry making. They are made of polished stainless steel and come with a sturdy construction in conjunction with housing, double springs for ease of use and comfortable, easy-to-handle colored foam handles. The round nose pliers are ideal for bending curves and curves in plates and wires.

- Snipe Nose Plier

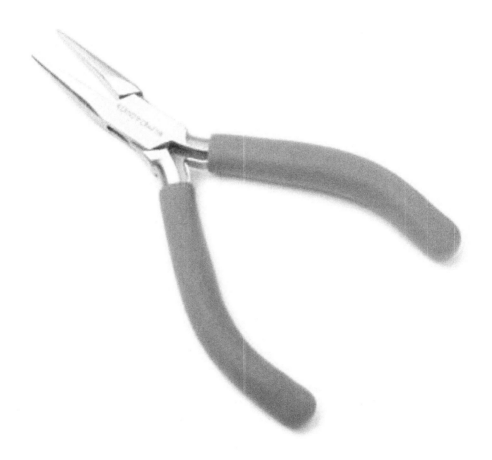

These jewelry pliers are ideal for most jewelry needs and are essential for all types of jewelry making. They are made of polished stainless steel and come with a sturdy construction in conjunction with housing, double springs for ease of use and comfortable, easy-to-handle colored foam handles. The fine-tipped pliers (sometimes called the chain tip) are a great general-purpose plier for bending metal sheets and wires and their narrow conical jaws to a fine point, making them useful for closing clamps in difficult to reach places. catch up.

- Flat-nose pliers

These flat-tipped jewelry pliers are ideal for most jewelry needs and are essential for all types of jewelry making. They are made of polished stainless steel and come with a sturdy construction in conjunction with housing, double springs for ease of use and comfortable, easy-to-handle colored foam handles. The flat-nose pliers have a wide, flat claw, making them ideal for grasping wider surfaces, bending angles in metal plates and wires, and for opening and closing jump rings.

- Nylon flat-nose pliers

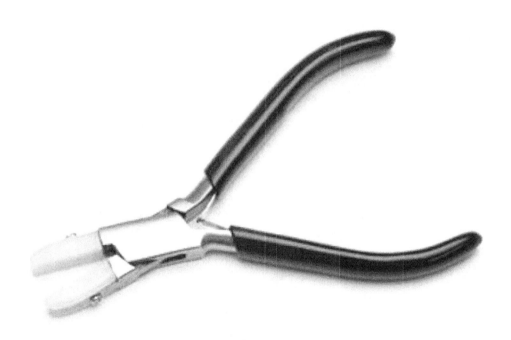

Nylon jaws and are ideal for working with threads and parts, as they do not damage, mark, or scratch the thread. Unlike the claws of ordinary pliers, the nylon claws of this plier protect the wire from scratches and dents, especially when opening and closing large jump rings or using wire winding techniques. These pliers are particularly useful for straightening wires too! They are hinged box construction for ease of use and nylon claws can be easily replaced when needed.

- Half-round pliers for ring bending pliers

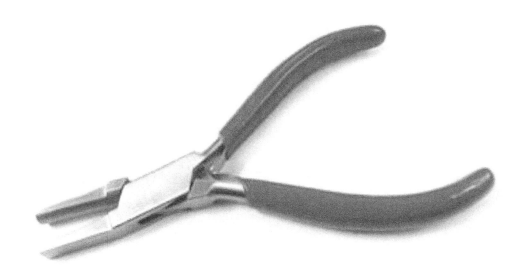

pliers to bend rings or half-round pliers are a great way to bend curves quickly and easily in sheet metal and flat wire or D-shaped.

One jaw has a semi-round cross-section to bend and form and the other jaw is flat, which helps to avoid marking the metal, so you can work gradually, bending, and shaping it as you go until you get a shape full ring. They are also useful for making headphones, as well as for other wired jobs.

- Side Cutters

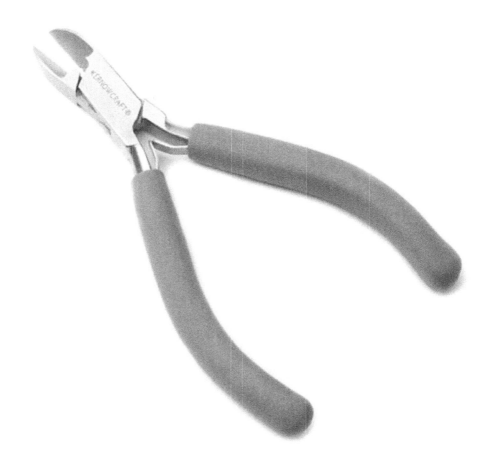

Side cutters are an essential and affordable tool for cutting and trimming precious metal wires, headpins, eye pins, etc. with minimal effort.

Please note that they are not suitable for cutting memory wires as they are made from very strong steel, which is why I always recommend other heavy-duty side cutters.

HAMMERS - CREATING TEXTURE AND WORK HARDENING

- Chasing Hammer

this hammer is good for directly hitting metal plates and wires on a steel block, anvil, sandbag, or stake to form complex curved and bent shapes. The rounded edge can also be used to obtain a hammered texture.

- Hammer Jeweler

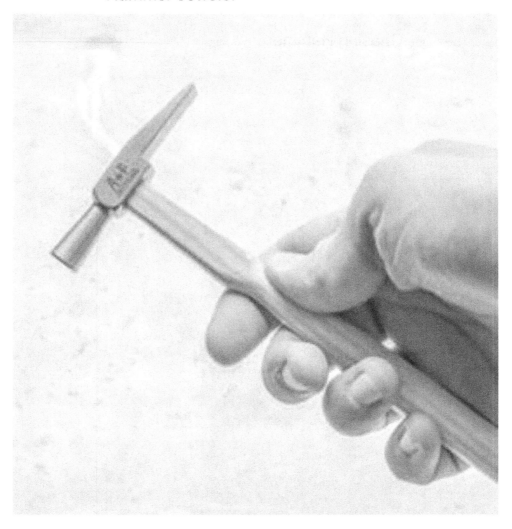

In addition to being ideal for driving and spreading rivets, it can also be used for fine-tuning jewelry shapes and for flattening thin threads. The end of the chisel can also be used to create a beautiful, peeling effect on the bark.

- Rawhide Mallet

The rawhide hammer is essential in the jewelry shop, as it is the best hammer for shaping and forming metal without leaving hammer marks. Use it in conjunction with a triblet or mandrel to smoothly shape and stretch rings and bracelets and to form metal shapes, where the use of a metal hammer creates a lot more finishing work due to the marks it inevitably leaves behind. On the other hand, it is also invaluable for the formation and application of textured metallic shapes, in which hammering can damage the surface.

- Mandrill Ring

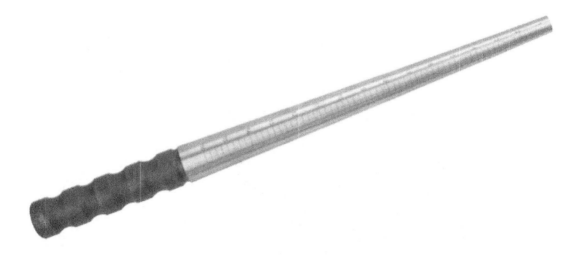

The chuck can be held in the hand and rotated while hammering or the handle at the bottom can be attached to the hand vise if you prefer. Always use a rawhide hammer to hammer your rings here, as this will not mark your pieces as a metal hammer would.

- Snipe Files To Smooth Edges

Ideal for precise and controlled archiving of metal and are small enough to reach hard-to-reach places, ideal for the complex work associated with jewelry making, as well as precision engineering and modeling.

- Gemstones and Beads

At this point, you should know well the pros and cons of each type of wire and the benefits of different types of pliers. Now, all you need is something to wrap. Gemstones and beads are acceptable centerpieces for your wire wrapping. Many stores sell beads in bulk at reasonably cheap prices - about $ 5 for a large bag. The beads are large enough to be wrapped and, depending on the nature of your project, many do not necessarily have to match. They are a simpler centerpiece, but still beautiful. On the other hand, gemstones are more expensive, but also more attractive to admirers.

WIRE WRAPPING TECHNIQUES

Materials:

- Center drilled hole Bead
- Head Pins

STEPS

1. Tie a bead or beads to a headpin.

2. Cut off the headpin, leaving 3/8 ".

3. Bend the wire at the top of the cord to a 90 ° angle with snipe nose pliers or your fingers.

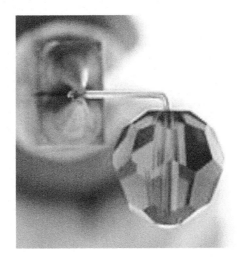

4. Hold the end of the wire with round-nose pliers so that it is level with the tool.

5. Rotate the pliers to form a loop.

6. Continue spinning the wire until it forms a complete loop.

7. To open the loop, hold the side of the loop closest to the opening with snipe nose pliers and move that side towards you.

8. Attach the loop to the desired location. To close the loop, hold the open side with snipe nose pliers and

move away from you until the loop is closed and the
end of the wire is flush with the base of the loop.

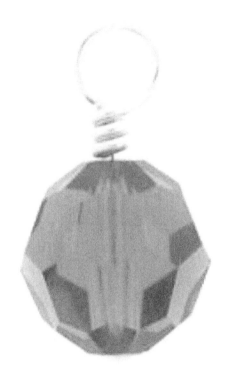

A wire-wrapped loop is one of the safest ways to connect beads and discoveries.

Materials:

- Center drilled hole Bead
- Head Pins

STEPS

1. Tie a bead or beads to the head pin. Remember to have at least an inch of wire over the last bead.

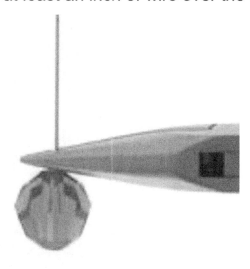

2. Using the tips of the chain nose pliers, take the wire directly above the beads.

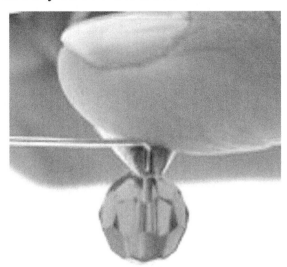

3. With your finger, push the wire at a 90 ° angle.

4. Using the round nose pliers, hold the wire in the curve.

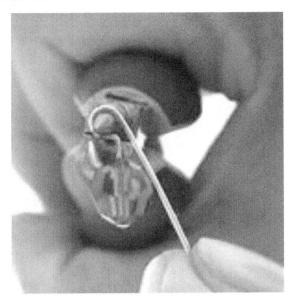

5. Pull the wire around the round nose pliers until it is almost pointing straight down.

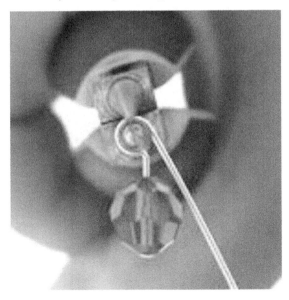

6. Reposition the pliers by opening the round-nose pliers (but do not pull the pliers out of the loop) and rotate the pliers so that the bottom tip is at the top.

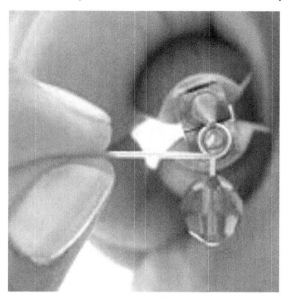

7. Continue stretching the wire around the nose of the pliers till the loop is fully round.

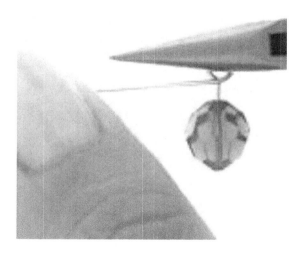

8. To wrap the loop, hold it with snipe-nose pliers and secure the wire with your fingers.

9. Wrap the wire around the head pin. Continue to wrap the cord around the cord.

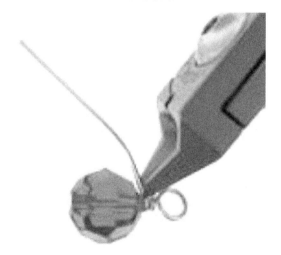

10. Using the pliers, cut the extra wire as close to the beads as possible.

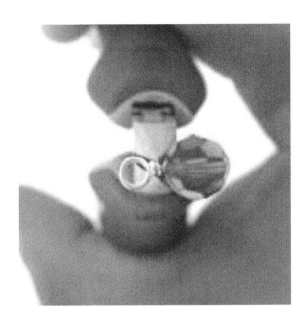

11. Secure the remaining end of the wire with the snipe nose pliers so that there are no sharp pieces of wire that could trap the clothing.

CHAPTER 5: WIRE WRAPPED LINK

Create unique jewelry with wire wrapped link techniques. Using wrapped link techniques, you can combine beads, chains, clasps, premade links, and more to create necklaces, bracelets, and earrings.

Materials:

- Center drilled hole bead - Swarovski Crystal Pearl Beads Chain
- Wire - Sterling Silver 22-gauge

STEPS

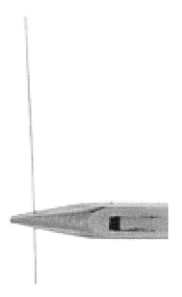

1. Hold the wire about 2.5 cm from the top with the snipe nose pliers.

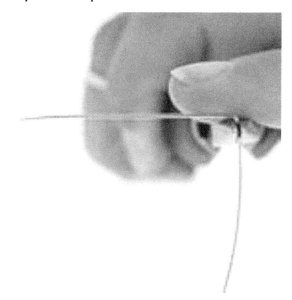

2. With your finger, push the wire at a 90 ° angle.

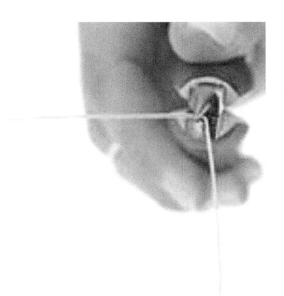

3. Using the round nose pliers, hold the wire in the curve.

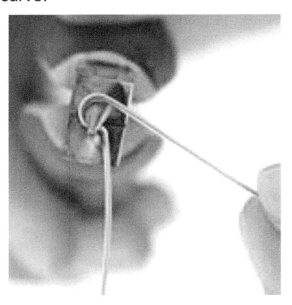

4. Pull the wire around the round nose pliers until it is almost pointing straight down.

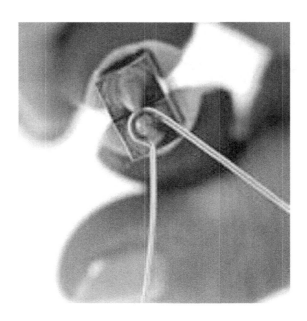

5. Reposition the pliers by opening the round-nose pliers (but do not pull the pliers out of the loop) and rotate the pliers so that the bottom tip is at the top.

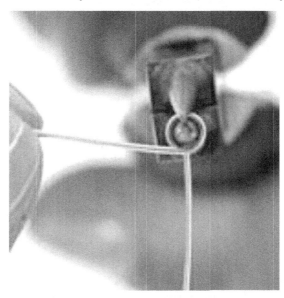

6. Endure pulling the wire around the nose of the pliers till the loop is fully round.

7. Attach a link or a chain to the loop.

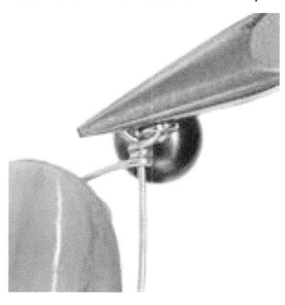

8. To wrap the loop, hold it with snipe-nose pliers and tighten the wire with your fingers.

9. Wrap the short wire around the long wire about 3 turns.

10. Using the pliers, cut the extra wire as close as possible.

11. Secure the remaining end of the wire with the snipe nose pliers so that there are no sharp pieces of wire that could trap the clothing.

12. Slide a bead or beads on the string.

13. Using the tips of the snipe nose pliers, take the wire directly above the beads.

14. With your finger, push the wire at a 90 ° angle.

15. Using the round nose pliers, hold the wire in the curve.

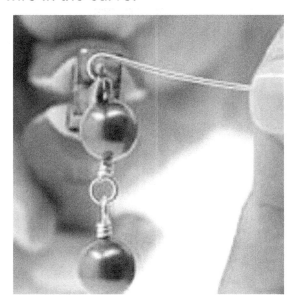

16. Pull the wire around the round nose pliers until it is almost pointing straight down.

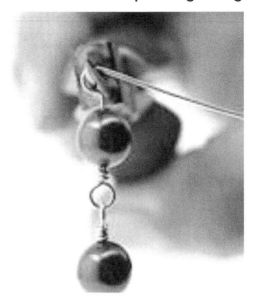

17. Reposition the pliers by opening the round nose pliers (but do not pull the pliers out of the loop) and rotate the pliers so that the bottom tip is at the top.

18. Keep on pulling the wire around the nose of the pliers till the loop is perfectly round.

19. Attach a link or a chain to the loop.

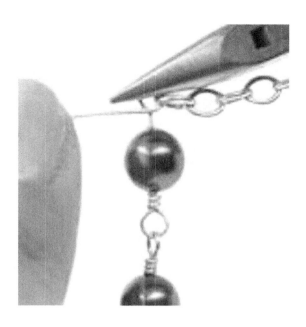

20. To wrap the loop, hold it with snipe nose pliers and secure the wire with your fingers.

21. Wrap the wire around the base wire. Continue wrapping the bead with the wire.

22. Using the cutter to cut the extra wire as close to the beads as possible.

23. Tuck the leftover tip of the wire with the snipe nose pliers so that there are no sharp pieces

of wire that could trap the clothing.

Add a wire wrapped look to a briolette bead. This technique will allow you to use your briolette and drop beads in the form of pendants on necklaces, bracelets, and earrings.

Materials:

- Top drilled hole Bead - briolette
- Wire - Sterling Silver 24 gauge

STEPS

1. Cut a 10 cm piece of wire. Slide the wire through the hole in the bead, leaving about 1 cm on the left side.

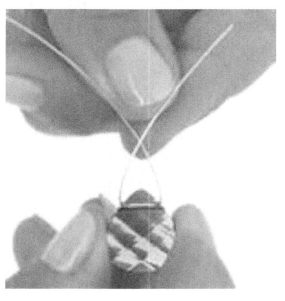

2. With your fingers, raise the wire there creating an intercept of the wires. The short piece should be in front of the longest side.

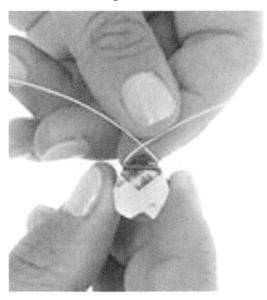

3. Using your fingers, bend the wire toward the briolette.

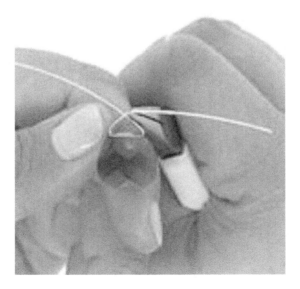

4. Use the tips of the snipe nose pliers to grip the small piece of wire directly above where the wires intersect.

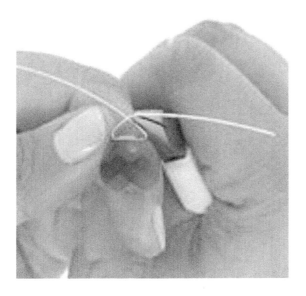

5. Bend the wire to a 90 ° angle.

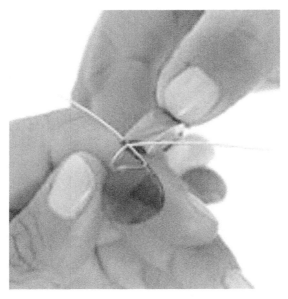

6. Use the tips of the snipe nose pliers to grip the longest piece of wire directly above where the wires intersect.

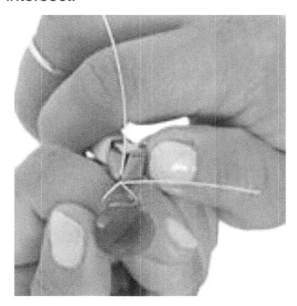

7. Fold the wire upward, forming a 90 ° angle between the two pieces of wire.

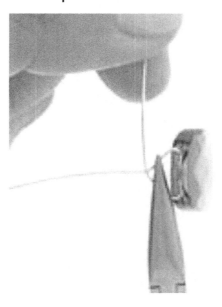

8. Hold the triangle that was created with the snipe nose pliers.

9. Wrap the short piece of wire around the longest piece about 1 1/2 - 2 wrap.

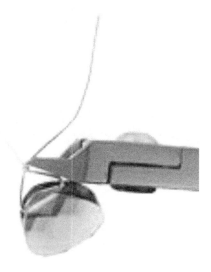

10. Use your cutter to cut the tail short as close as possible.

11. Using the tips of the snipe nose pliers, take the wire directly above the wrap.

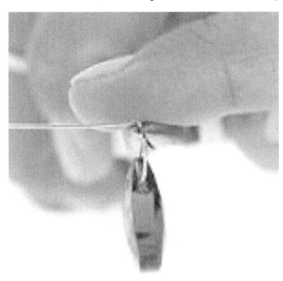

12. With your finger, push the wire at a 90 ° angle.

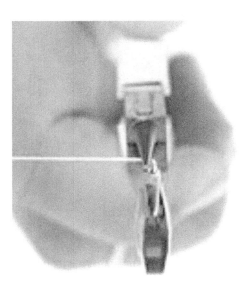

13. Using the round nose pliers, hold the wire in the curve.

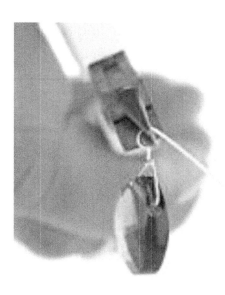

14. Pull the wire around the round nose pliers until it is almost pointing straight down.

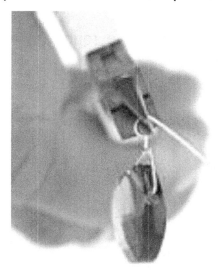

15. Reposition the pliers by opening the round nose pliers (but do not pull the pliers out of the

loop) and rotate the pliers so that the bottom tip is at the top.

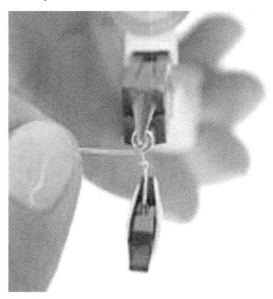

16. Keep pulling the wire around the nose of the pliers till the loop is perfectly round.

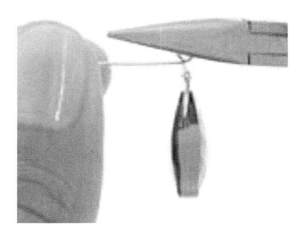

17. If you are attaching it to a chain or ring, this is a good time. To wrap the loop, hold it with snipe nose pliers and grip the wire with your fingers.

18. Wrap the wire around the base wire. Keep looping the wire until the first wrap.

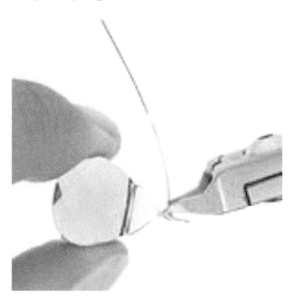

19. Using the cutter to cut the extra wire as close to the wrap as possible.

20. Nice, you have now created a wire wrapped triangle pendant!

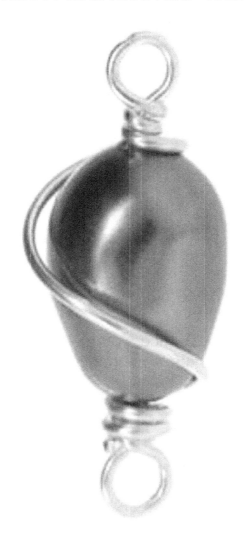

Create an elegant, spiraled ornament with wire, wrapping it around your favorite bead!

Materials:

- Bead with a center drilled hole
- Wire - dead soft sterling silver 22-gauge

STEPS

1. Cut a 10 cm piece of wire. Create a wire wrapped loop at the wire extreme.

2. Tie a bead on the wire.

3. Make a loop around the other side of the bead.

4. Wrap the wire up to the cord.

5. Bring the wire back and forth over the bead, continuing the winding movement.

73

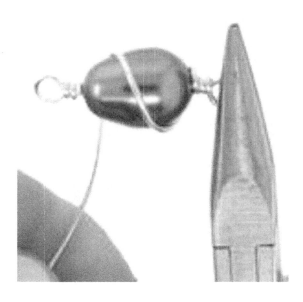

6. Continue to wind the bead until you reach the first coiled wire.

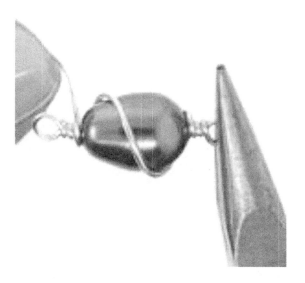

7. Wrap the wire once around the bottom of the first wire wrap.

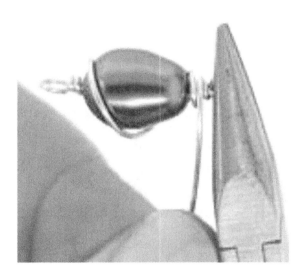

8. Keep winding the wire back around the first wire wrap. It can help to hold the first loop with chain nose pliers.

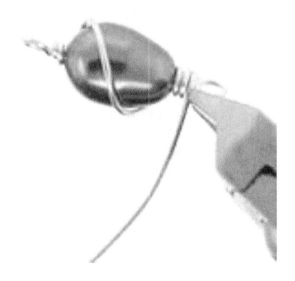

9. After completely winding the first wire wrap, use cutters to cut the excess wire.

10. Use snipe nose pliers to tighten and bind the end of the wire firmly to the wire wrap, so that the wire does not peel off and pinch clothing.

11. Congratulations! You now have a wire wrapped around a bead.

This process will teach you how to wrap wire over the head of your favorite bead to make a bail and bead cap all in one.

Materials:

- Bead with center drilled hole
- Long head pin - 24 gauge 3 inch head pin

STEPS

1. Start a basic wire wrap by tying a bead or beads to the head pin. Leave at least 2 inches of wire above the last bead.

2. Using the tips of the snipe/chain nose pliers, take the wire directly above the last bead.

3. With your finger, push the wire at a 90 ° angle.

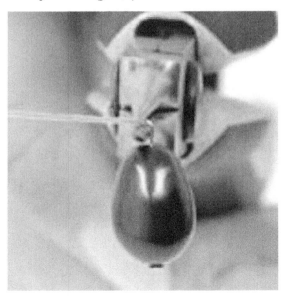

4. Using the round nose pliers, hold the wire in the curve.

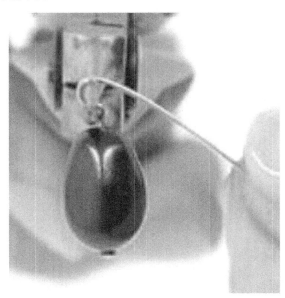

5. Pull the wire around the round nose pliers until it is almost pointing straight down.

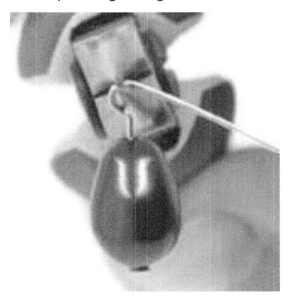

6. Reposition the pliers by opening the round-nose pliers (but do not pull the pliers out of the loop) and rotate the pliers so that the bottom tip is at the top.

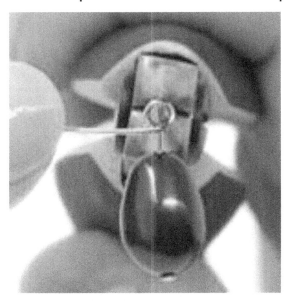

7. Keep pulling the wire around the nose of the pliers till the loop is fully round.

8. To wrap the loop, hold it with snipe-nose pliers and grip the end of the wire with your fingers.

9. Wrap the wire around the head pin. Keep wrapping the wire around the bead as you would do for a basic wrap.

10. After finishing the basic wire wrapping, start making the cover by wrapping the wire around the last wrap.

11. Again, make another wrap around that of step 10. Use the wrap from step 10 to form corresponding. This will make your second bead cover wrap.

12. Stop wrapping when you have a large-cap as you may want. For this technique, we chose to go for three wraps.

13. Use the cutter to trim the excess wire as close to the beads as possible.

This involves you wrapping wire over the top of a briolette to makes an elegant bail.

Materials:

- Briolette/Tear drop bead with top-drilled
- Wire Used - 26/24 gauge gold-filled wire - dead soft or sterling silver

STEPS

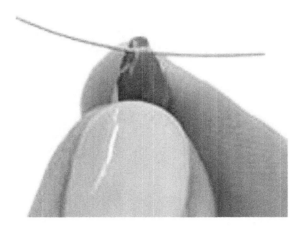

1. Pass a wire through your briolette.

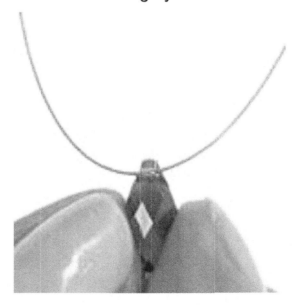

2. Place the briolette to the middle of the wire.

3. Pull both sides of the wire upwards - forming the wire on the sides of the briolette hole.

4. Use the spine/chain nose pliers to carefully tighten the two pieces of wire. The wires must be parallel to

each other. This will form a small triangle around the top of the briolette.

5. Hold the two wires with the spine/chain nose pliers just above the tip of the briolette.

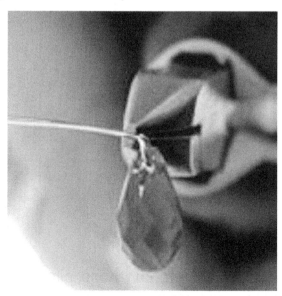

6. Bend the pliers until the wires are at the right angle shape.

7. Using the round nose pliers, hold the wires in the bend.

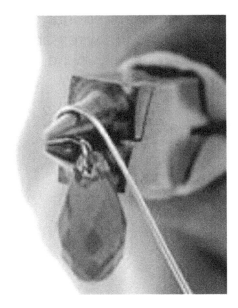

8. Pull the wires around the round nose pliers until they are almost pointing straight down.

9. Reposition the pliers by opening the round-nose pliers (but do not pull the pliers out of the loop) and rotate the pliers so that the bottom tip is at the top. Keep pulling the wires around the nose of the pliers till the loop is fully round.

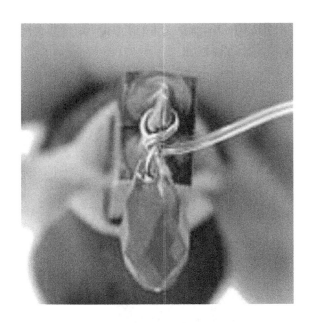

10. If you are attaching a chain or ear wire, kindly attach before proceeding to the next step.

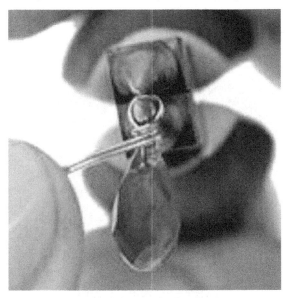

11. To wrap the loop, continue holding the loop with the round-nose pliers and hold the wires

with your fingers. Pull the wires around the neck of the triangle bail.

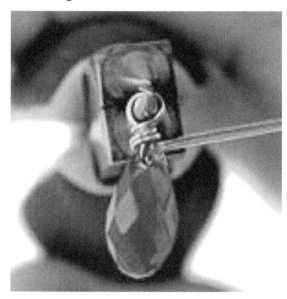

12. Strain the wires back in front of your briolette. The wires must be parallel to each other.

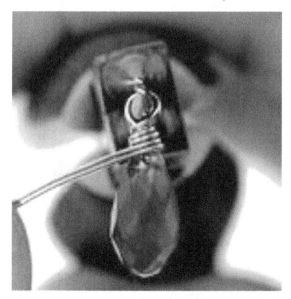

13. Re-pull the wires around the back of the briolette and ensures the wires are parallel to each other.

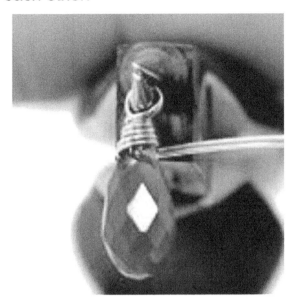

14. Continue to strand the wires around the briolette.

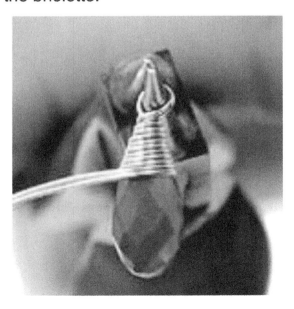

15. Stop wrapping the wires when you have covered the briolette as desired.

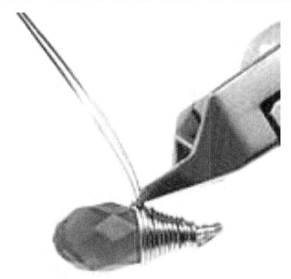

16. Use the cutter to trim the wires as close as possible to the briolette. Congratulations! You have successfully wrap a briolette!

Materials:

- Bead with a center drilled hole
- Wire Used - 26-gauge sterling silver wire

STEPS

1. Cut a 15 to 16 " of wire. Create a wrapped loop around one end. Wrap the wire round by doubling the number of wraps you want in the herringbone weave. For this guide, we are creating 10 wrapped coils that are equivalent to 5 wraps around the bead. Refer to the wire-wound link technique earlier did.

2. Tie a bead on the wire.

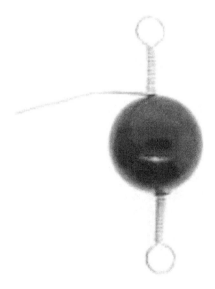

3. Repeat Step 1 for the other end of your wire. Ensure there is a uniform number of wraps on both sides of the bead. We have 10 wrapped coils on both sides.

So do not cut the end of the wire, you will use it to make the design all through.

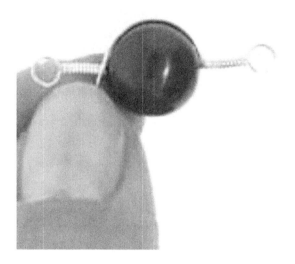

4. To start the herringbone wrapping, form the wire around one side of the bead. Place the wire over the first wrapped coil.

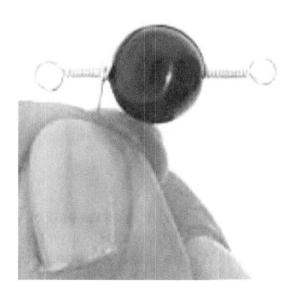

5. Create a wrap around the wrapped coil.

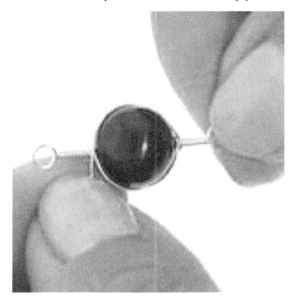

6. Form the wire behind the wire of the opposite side of the bead. Place the wire over the second wrapped coil.

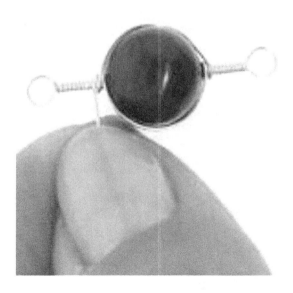

7. Create a wrap around the wrapped coil.

8. Form the wire behind the wire on the first side of the bead. Place the wire over the wrapped coil.

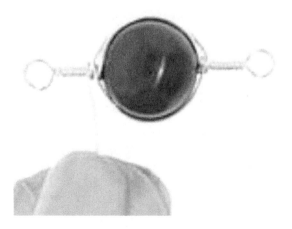

9. Create a wrap around the wrapped coil.

10. Make the wire behind the wire on the second side of the bead. Place the wire over the wrapped coil.

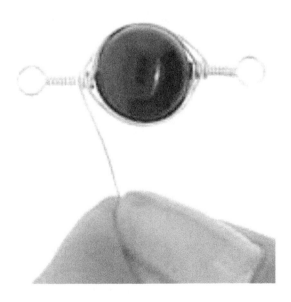

11. Create a wrap around the wrapped coil.

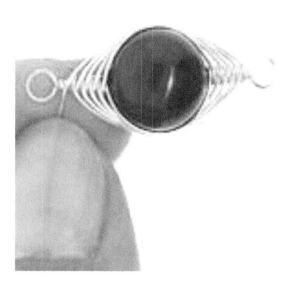

12. Keep repeating the pattern until you reach the tip of the coil. Now, you have created 5 herringbone wraps.

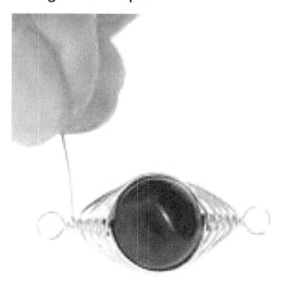

13. To secure, make an extra wrap around the wrapped coil.

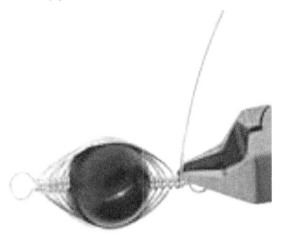

14. Using wire cutters, cut the end of your wire.

15. Make more links of herringbone wire and tie them to a necklace, bracelet, or earrings. Also, try to link them with wire wrapped links.

Materials:

- 1 x 130cts Black Spinel Graduated Plain Drops Approx 8 to 12mm, 25cm Strand.
- 1 x 50m Gold Plated Copper Wire 0.4mm
- 1 x 10m Gold Plated Copper Wire 1mm
- 1 x Gold Color Plated Copper Open Jump Rings ID Approx 7mm. (Approx 200pcs).

STEPS

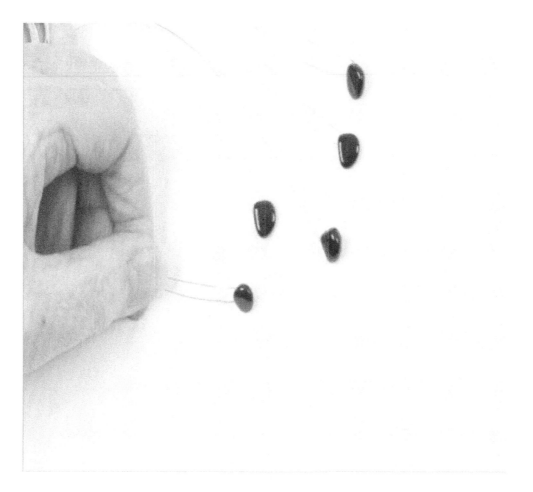

1. Cut 5 x 20 cm of 0.4 mm wire and place it through the middle of each length.

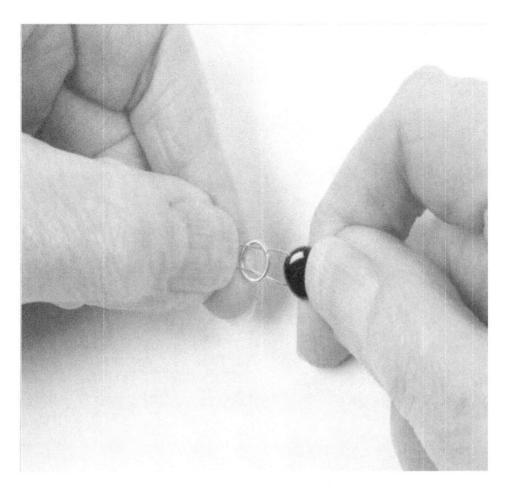

2. Take a 7 mm jump ring and pass both ends of the wire through the middle

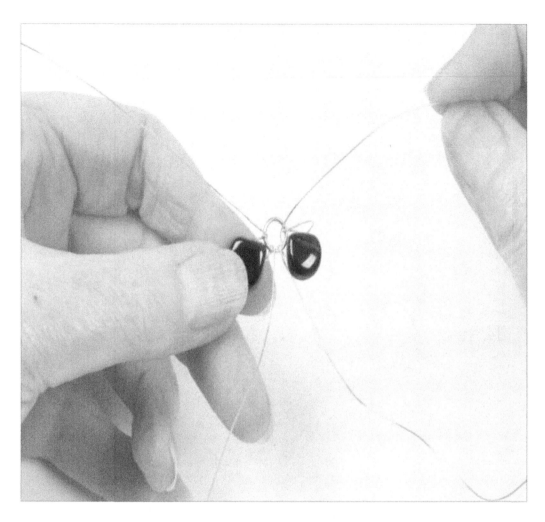

3. Holding the drop in place, wrap each length of wire around the jump ring a few times. Repeat with the 4 drops leaving all the long tips intact for later use.

4. Add an 8 mm round cord to one of the lengths and drop it to cover the jump ring, secure the end by wrapping it around the jump ring a few times.

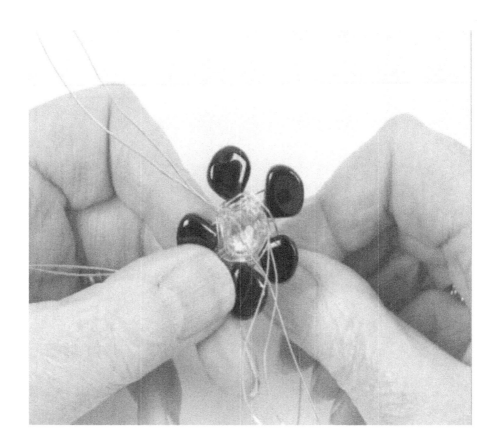

5. Leave 2 lengths of wire opposite each other for later use to attach to the ring stem. Use the remaining lengths of the wire to weave in and out of the stones, creating a basket weaving impression and protecting the stones.

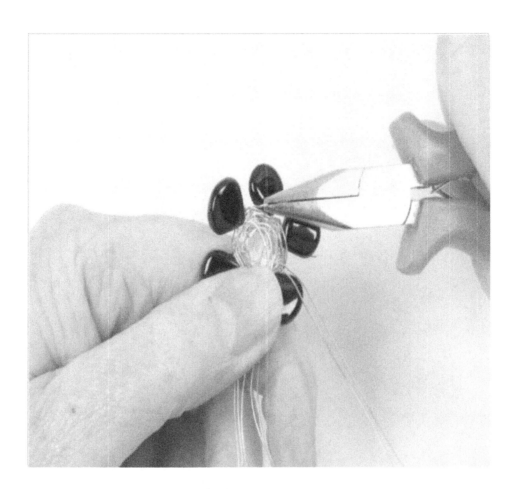

6. When the weaving is complete, trim the ends and bend them using flat-nose pliers.

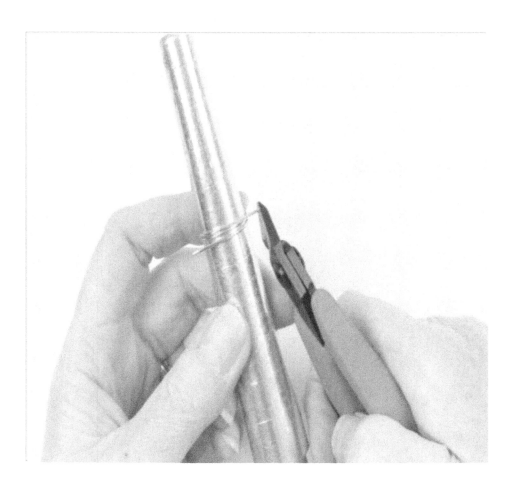

7. Take a 25 cm long 1.00 mm wire and place the center in a ring mandrel. Without crossing the wires, wrap each end around the mandrel and trim each end approximately 1 cm.

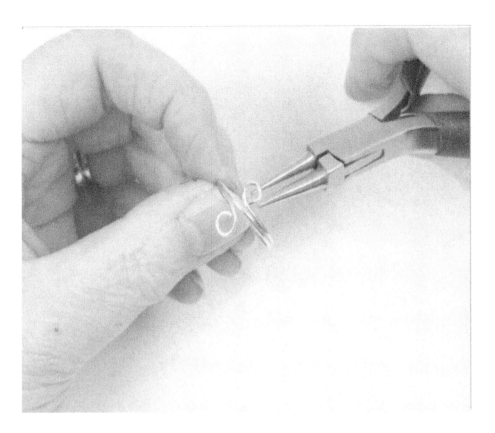

8. Using round-nose pliers, loop in opposite directions at each 1 cm end.

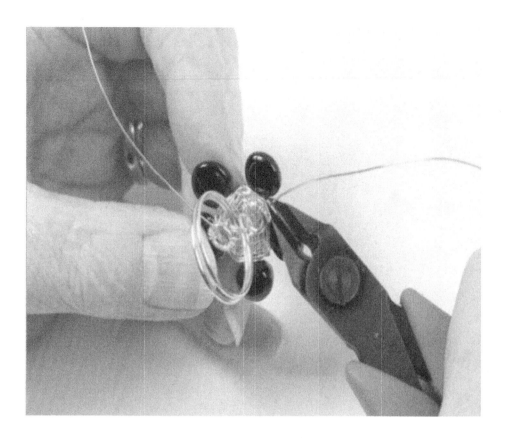

9. Using the 0.4 mm wire lengths saved earlier, hold the flower in place over the handles of the ring stem and grasp it by wrapping each wire around the handles a few times. Trim the ends and bend them using flat-nose pliers.

CHAPTER 12: WIRE WRAP CABOCHON PENDANT

Materials:

- 1 x Cabochon
- Bronze wire - 0.4mm
- Copper wire - 1.0mm

STEPS

1. Start by cutting 3 lengths of 1 mm wire, long enough to wrap around the entire cabochon you are about to work on and surplus to pay the bail. This cabochon is large and we cut a wire length of about 50 cm in length.

2. Holding the 3 lengths of wire tightly together and side by side and using the 0.4 mm, grasp the 3 wires together with a few bands by pressing each winding with the flat-nose pliers as you go. Trim the ends of the wrapping wire from the same side so that they are hidden against the cabochon.

3. Place the cabochon on the table and holding the wrapped area against the bottom of the cabochon, push the two middle wires around the edge of the cabochon, bring them to the top and leave a space of approximately ½ cm. flat-nose pliers and fold it upwards (they make up 2 of 4 wires that will be used to bail).

4. Crises crosses the two wires in front of the cabochon.

5. Working now at the back of the cabochon, bring the two wires at the back and cross them as we did at the front, where the wires meet, use the flat-nose pliers fold the two wires upwards (these will be the other 2 of 4 wires) used to post bail).

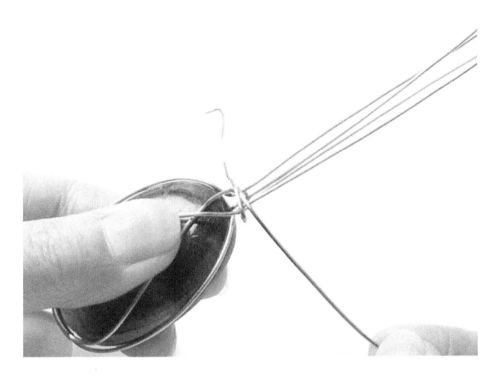

6. Hold all the wires at the top of the cabochon with your thumb on the front cross wires and the front finger holding the two rear wires, take each front wire and wrap it around the base of the 4 wires that we will use to form the bail. safe.

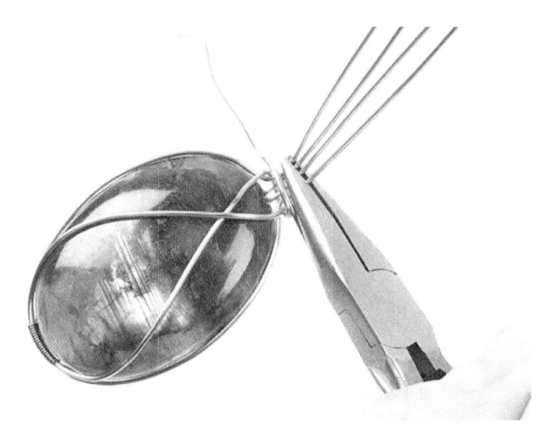

7. With the flat-nose pliers, slightly bend the four wires of the bail.

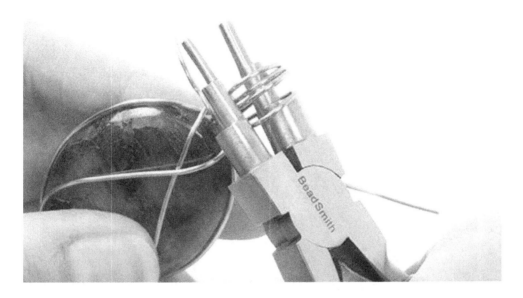

8. Using the widest part of the pliers, place it behind the bail wires and create the bail by pushing the four wires over the pliers and backing up at the back of the cabochon.

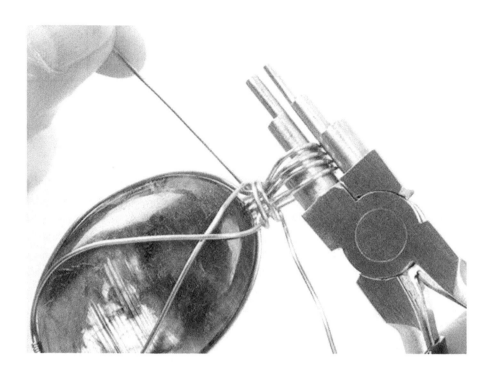

9. Grasp the bail by wrapping it a few times with the wires previously used, cut off the excess wire, and tuck the ends so they are not pointed.

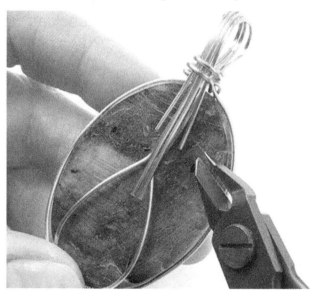

10. Trim the wires at the back of the cabochon, as shown.

11. With round-nose pliers, loop each end of the wires to look neat.

12. You can hang the pendant from a popcorn chain, chain, or leather cord to complete the necklace.

Made in the USA
Las Vegas, NV
09 February 2024

85575668R00083